A Crabtree Branches Book

SERVING
with Honor

ARMY

written by **Bernard Conaghan**

CRABTREE
Publishing Company
www.crabtreebooks.com

School-to-Home Support for Caregivers and Teachers

This high-interest book is designed to motivate striving students with engaging topics while building fluency, vocabulary, and an interest in reading. Here are a few questions and activities to help the reader build upon his or her comprehension skills.

Before Reading:
- *What do I think this book is about?*
- *What do I know about this topic?*
- *What do I want to learn about this topic?*
- *Why am I reading this book?*

During Reading:
- *I wonder why...*
- *I'm curious to know...*
- *How is this like something I already know?*
- *What have I learned so far?*

After Reading:
- *What was the author trying to teach me?*
- *What are some details?*
- *How did the photographs and captions help me understand more?*
- *Read the book again and look for the vocabulary words.*
- *What questions do I still have?*

Extension Activities:
- *What was your favorite part of the book? Write a paragraph on it.*
- *Draw a picture of your favorite thing you learned from the book.*

Table of Contents

Mission

The United States Army is one branch of the United States Armed Forces. It is responsible for **military operations** on land to keep the U.S. safe.

Values

Soldiers are expected to live by values. They are loyalty, duty, respect, selfless service, honor, **integrity**, and personal courage. The seven core Army values guide soldiers' actions every day whether on or off the job. The Soldier's Creed is an **oath** to these values.

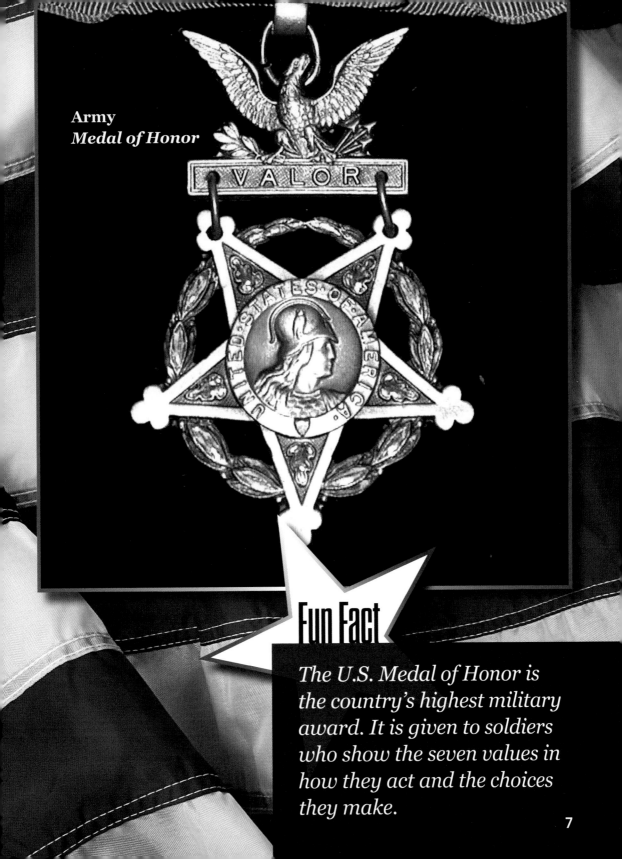

Army
Medal of Honor

VALOR

UNITED·STATES·OF·AMERICA·

Fun Fact

The U.S. Medal of Honor is the country's highest military award. It is given to soldiers who show the seven values in how they act and the choices they make.

Every service member must say the Oath of Enlistment. Officers say the military oath of office. This is a promise to defend the **U.S. Constitution**.

Uniform

The Army has strict rules for uniforms. Combat uniforms have **camouflage** and are easy to work in. Service uniforms have a button-up shirt. They can be worn every day. Dress or "mess" uniforms are the most formal. These are worn on special occasions.

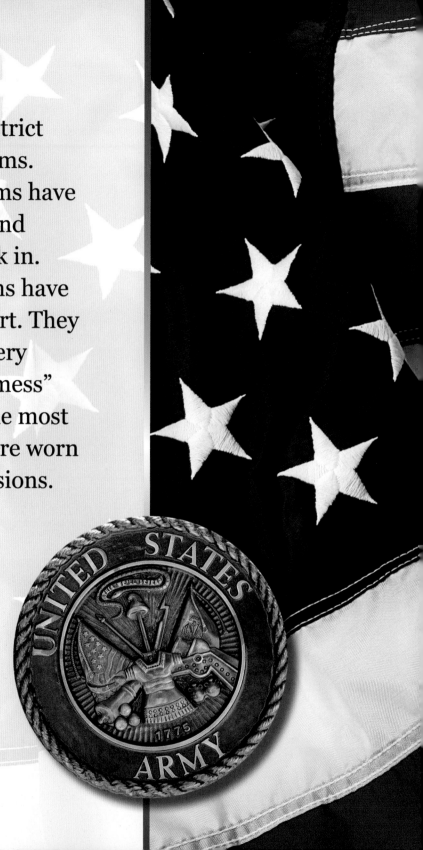

Fun Fact

Army "pinks and greens" were used in World War II and the Korean War. The pink comes from the pink hue of the taupe khaki pants and skirts.

Equipment and Vehicles

Special vehicles and equipment are used to complete **missions** on land. The main battle **tank** used is the M1 Abrams. The High-Mobility Multipurpose Wheeled Vehicle (HMMWV), known as the Humvee, moves troops.

High-Mobility Multipurpose Wheeled Vehicle (HMMWV)

M1 Abrams

The U.S. Army also uses aircraft. The UH-60 Black Hawk is one of many helicopters in the fleet. Drones are used for surveillance and targeting missions.

UH-60 Black Hawk

RQ-11 Raven
unmanned drone

Fun Fact

The Modular Lightweight Load-carrying Equipment (MOLLE) system is used to carry gear and tools needed when going into the battlefield. It can be customized so a soldier only brings what is necessary.

Having the right equipment is important. Night vision goggles help soldiers see in the dark. **Satellites** transmit information. Laser target locators help find targets.

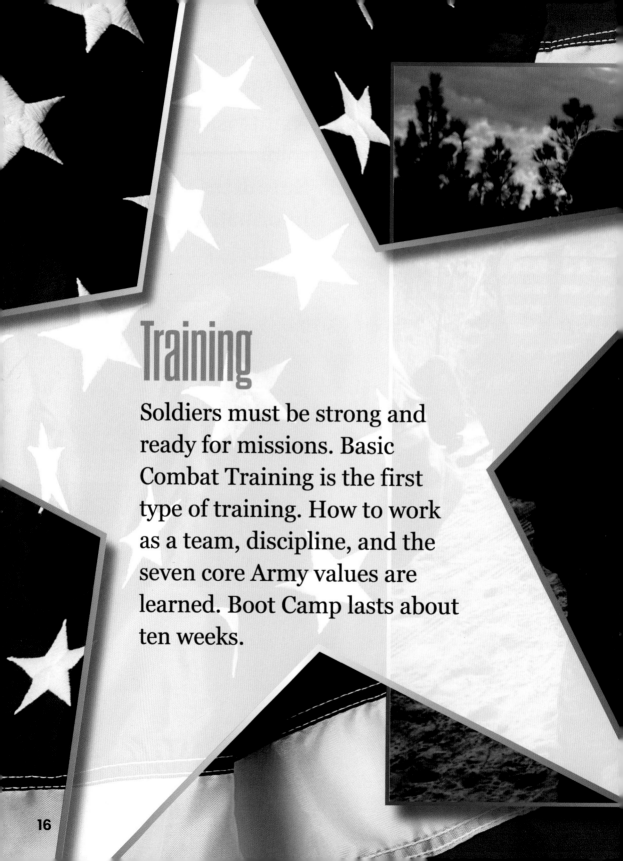

Training

Soldiers must be strong and ready for missions. Basic Combat Training is the first type of training. How to work as a team, discipline, and the seven core Army values are learned. Boot Camp lasts about ten weeks.

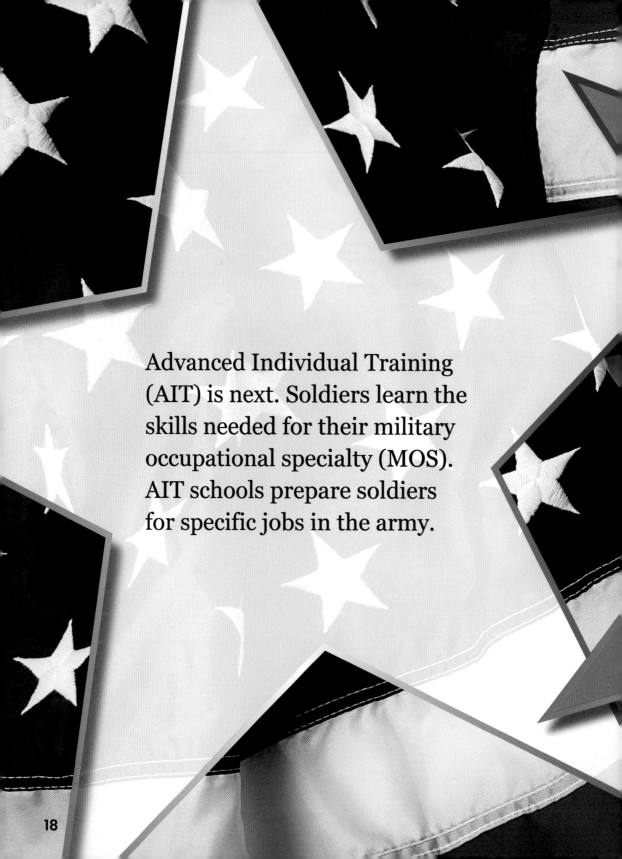

Advanced Individual Training (AIT) is next. Soldiers learn the skills needed for their military occupational specialty (MOS). AIT schools prepare soldiers for specific jobs in the army.

Careers

The U.S. Army has many different types of jobs for the battlefield. The Intelligence Analyst uses technology to give troops information about the enemy. The Armor Crewman drives the tanks and other armored vehicles.

Fun Fact

Many jobs in the army also prepare soldiers for jobs as **civilians**. *Some training allows soldiers to get a professional license from trade organizations.*

The U.S. Army also has jobs that provide support to the troops. Culinary specialists prepare and serve the food. Cargo specialists make sure that equipment, supplies, and mail arrive wherever the troops are located.

Keeping equipment working is important.
Electronics specialists repair electronics
and safely disarm explosives. Mechanics
keep vehicles running.

Ways to Serve

There are three main ways to serve in the U.S. Army. Active duty soldiers live and work on an Army base full-time. Soldiers in the Army Reserve serve part-time and can live anywhere in the U.S. The National Guard also serve part-time. They can be called by the state or federal government.

Army Reserve's top drill sergeant competition

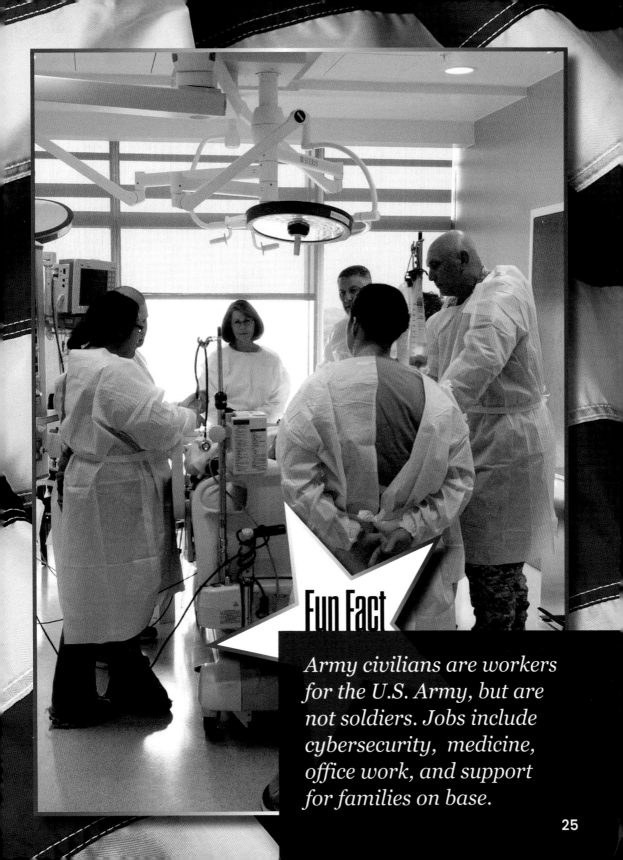

Fun Fact

Army civilians are workers for the U.S. Army, but are not soldiers. Jobs include cybersecurity, medicine, office work, and support for families on base.

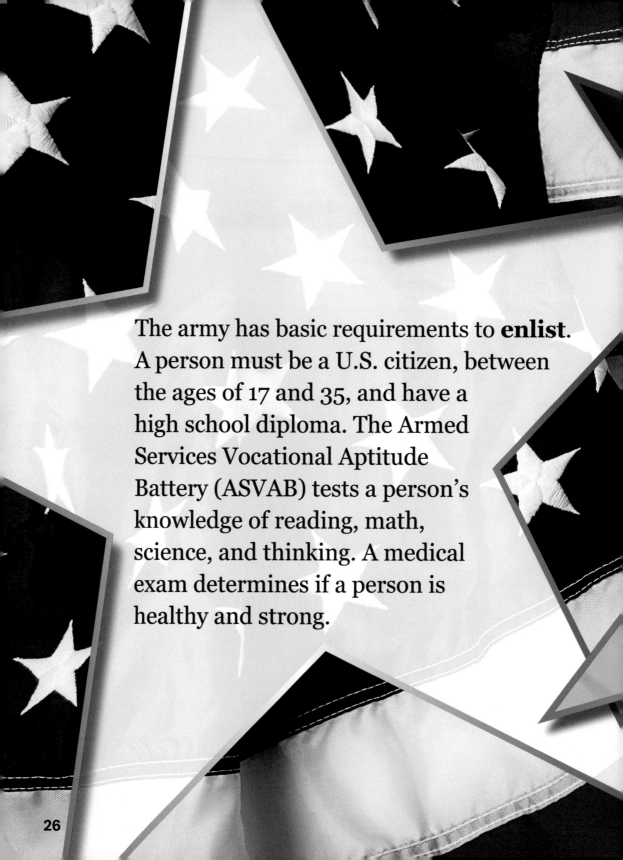

The army has basic requirements to **enlist**. A person must be a U.S. citizen, between the ages of 17 and 35, and have a high school diploma. The Armed Services Vocational Aptitude Battery (ASVAB) tests a person's knowledge of reading, math, science, and thinking. A medical exam determines if a person is healthy and strong.

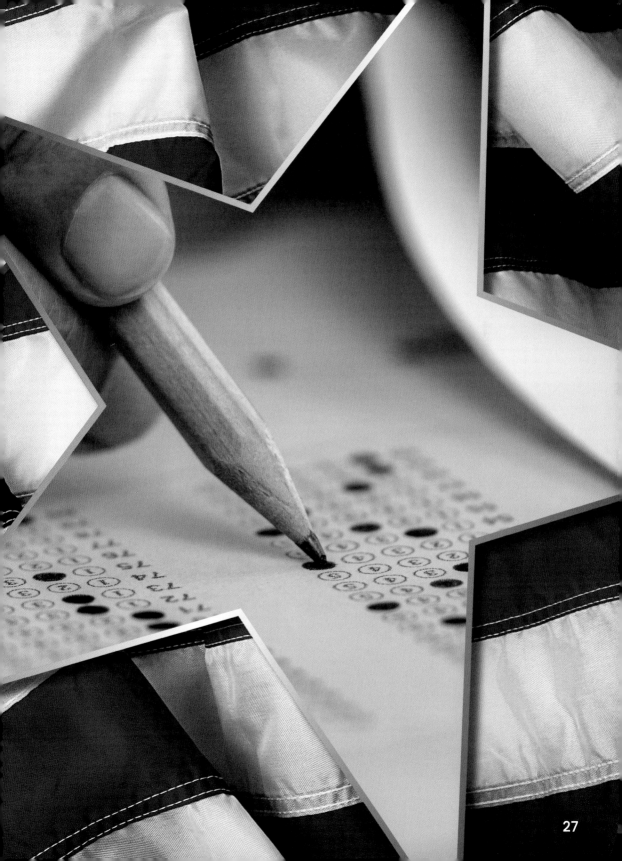

Showing Appreciation

Members of the army are on call every day of the year. They put their lives at risk to keep us safe. We celebrate them throughout the year. May is Military Appreciation month.

Thank You
HONORING ALL WHO SERVE

Veterans Day is a time to thank those who are serving. It is also for those who served in the past and are still living. Memorial Day is for remembering the men and women who lost their lives serving their country. Are you ready to serve in the U.S. Army?

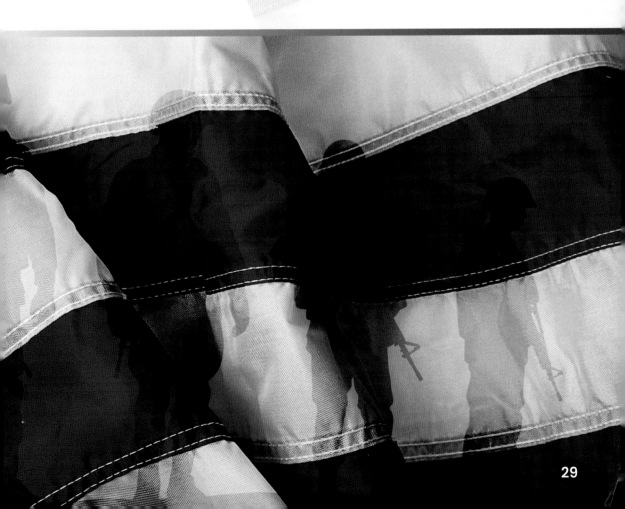

Glossary

camouflage (**ka**·muh·flaazh) Disguising items to help someone blend in with their surroundings

civilian (suh·**vi**·lyn) Someone who is not in the armed forces or police

enlist (uhn·**list**) To join the armed forces

integrity (uhn·**teh**·gruh·tee) Having strong morals

military operations (**mi**·luh·teh·ree aa·pr·**ay**·shnz) Armed actions in response to a situation

mission (**mi**·shn) An assignment

oath (owth) A promise

satellite (**sa**·tuh·lite) An item that is in Earth's orbit and communicates information

tank (tangk) Armored vehicle with weapons attached

U.S. Constitution (kaan·stuh·**too**·shn) The rights and laws that are the basis for the government of the United States

Index

Websites

www.army.mil
www.goarmy.com
www.militaryonesource.mil

About the Author

Bernard Conaghan lives in South Carolina with his German shepherd named Duke. His grandmother was the jeep driver for the Major General for the U.S. Marines during World War II. He is a coach on his son's football team. He always eats one scoop of peach ice cream after dinner.

CRABTREE
Publishing Company

Written by: Bernard Conaghan
Designed by: Jen Bowers
Proofreader: Petrice Custance
Print Coordinator: Katherine Berti

Photographs: Cover U.S. Army photo, U.S. flag ©2008 J. Helgason/Shutterstock; p.3 U.S. Army photo, p.5 U.S. Air Force photo/Staff Sgt. Dallas Edwards; p.6 U.S. Army photo/Sgt. Jose A. Torres Jr.; p.7 public domain image; p.9 U.S. Army photo/Spc. Brian A. Barbour; p.10 ©2010 Keith McIntyre/Shutterstock; p.11 Timothy L. Hale/Army Reserve Public Affairs; p.12 U.S. Army photo/Spc. Genesis Gomez, U.S. Army photo/Sgt. Todd Robinson; p.13 U.S. Army photo, U.S. Army photo/Sgt. Kimberly Trumbull; p.14 U.S. Army photo; p.15 Public Affairs/Maj. Daniel Markert, U.S. Army photo/Staff Sgt. Mark Burrel; p.17 U.S. Army photo/Staff Sgt. Shawn Weismiller; p.19 U.S. Army photo; p.20 U.S. Army photo; p.21 U.S. Army photo/Spc. Joanna N. Amberge; p.22 U.S. Army photo/T.Anthony Bell; p.23 U.S. Army photo/Sgt. Mike MacLeod; p.24 U.S. Army photo/Sgt. 1st Class Brian Hamilton; p.25 U.S. Army photo/Staff Sgt. Teddy Wade; p.27 ©2019 smolaw/Shutterstock; p.28-29 Black Creator 24/Shutterstock

Library and Archives Canada Cataloguing in Publication

Available at the Library and Archives Canada

Library of Congress Cataloging-in-Publication Data

Available at the Library of Congress

Crabtree Publishing Company
www.crabtreebooks.com   1-800-387-7650

Copyright © 2023 **CRABTREE PUBLISHING COMPANY**

Published in the United States
Crabtree Publishing
347 Fifth Avenue
Suite 1402-145
New York, NY, 10016

Published in Canada
Crabtree Publishing
616 Welland Ave.
St. Catharines, ON
L2M 5V6

Printed in the U.S.A./072022/CG20220201